Big Machines At Work

Cranes

By Hal Rogers

The Child's World® Inc. ◆ Eden Prairie, Minnesota

Published by The Child's World®, Inc.
7081 W. 192 Ave.
Eden Prairie, MN 55346

Design and Production:
The Creative Spark, San Juan Capistrano, CA

Photos: © 1998 David M. Budd Photography

Library of Congress Cataloging-in-Publication Data

Rogers, Hal, 1966-
    Cranes / by Hal Rogers.
        p. cm.
    Summary: Describes the parts of a crane, how it works, and the work it does
at a construction site.
    ISBN 1-56766-651-5 (lib. bdg. : alk. paper)
    1. Cranes, derricks, etc. Juvenile literature. [1. Cranes, derricks, etc.] I. Title.
TJ1363.R59 1999
621.8'73—dc21
                                                               99-20857
                                                                CIP

Contents

On the Job

On the job, cranes work at a **construction site.** A crane helps workers lift and move heavy objects.

The workers want to move a heavy block of concrete. The crane has a long metal **cable.** The workers attach the cable to the block.

The crane has a tall, strong arm. It is called a **boom.** The cable hangs from the boom.

The boom swings around very slowly. It carries the block to where the workers need it. It lowers the block down as the workers guide it.

This big, blue box is called the

crane house. There is a heavy

weight attached to it.

12

The weight helps keep the crane steady
as it lifts a heavy load.

Cranes do not have wheels. They use **crawler tracks** to move around the construction site.

There are many different kinds of cranes.

This one is shaped like the letter "T."

It has a very long boom. The boom can

reach far across the construction site.

Climb Aboard!

Would you like to see where the driver sits?

A crane driver is called an **operator.**

He uses special **levers** and **pedals** to make

the crane work.

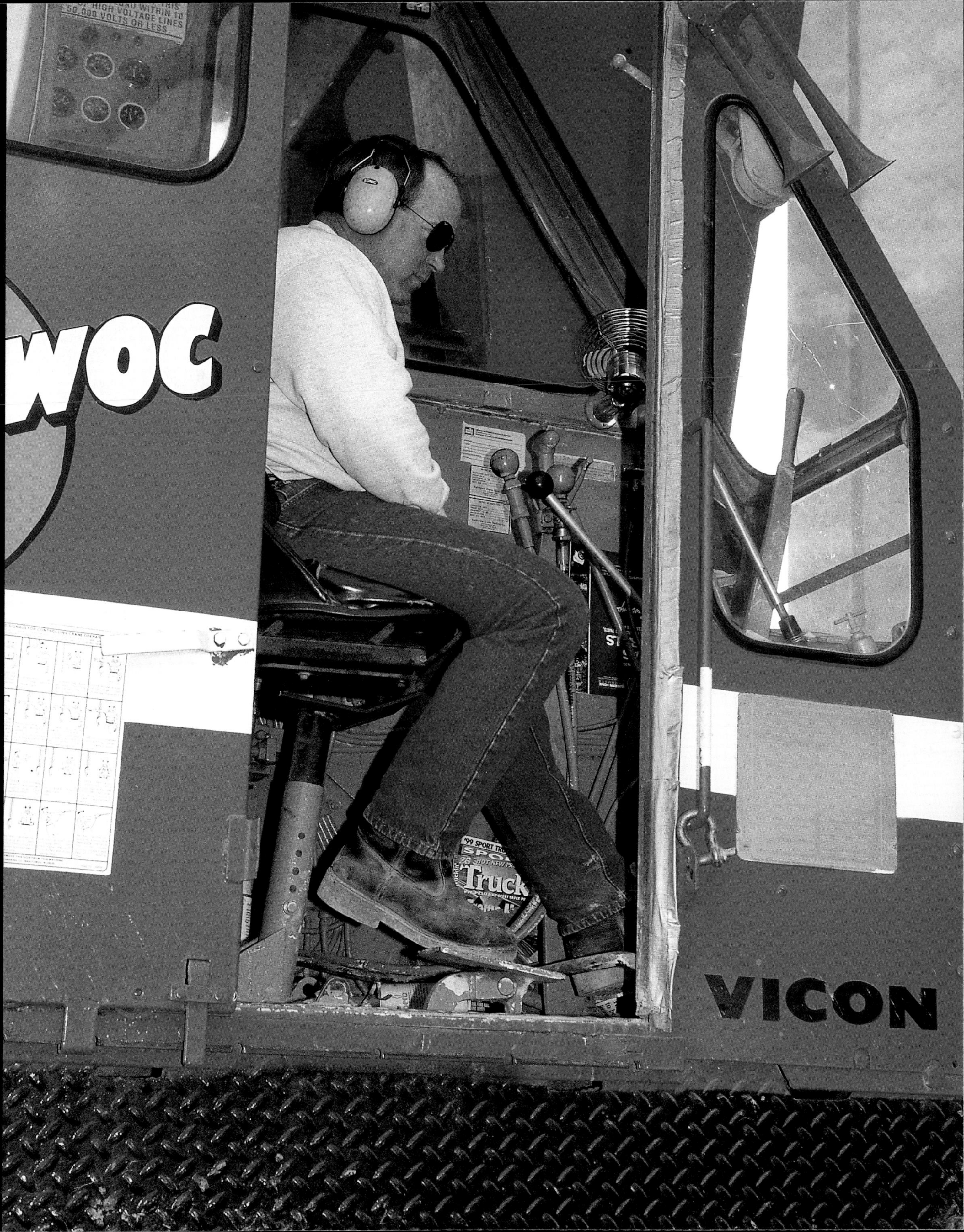
50,000 VOLTS OR LESS.
WOC
'99 SPORT TRUCK
Truck
VICON

Up Close

The inside

1. The operator's seat

2. The levers

3. The pedals

The outside

1. The crawler tracks

2. The crane house

3. The boom

4. The cable

5. The weight

Glossary

boom (BOOM)
The boom is the long arm on a crane. It swings around to move a heavy object.

cable (KAY-bull)
A cable is a strong rope made out of metal. A crane's cable picks up heavy objects.

construction site (kun-STRUCK-shun SITE)
A construction site is a place where workers build something. Workers make buildings at a construction site.

crane house (KRAYN HOWSE)
The crane house is the part of a crane where the operator sits. A large weight is attached to the crane house.

crawler tracks (KRAWL-er TRAX)
Crawler tracks are huge belts made of rubber and metal on a crane. They spin around to move a crane back and forth.

levers (LEV-ers)
Levers are metal bars with black knobs at the ends. The crane operator uses them to move a load.

operator (OPP-er-ay-ter)
The operator is the person who runs the crane. He or she makes the crane work.

pedals (PED-elz)
Pedals are levers that people can operate with their feet. Pedals help the operator use the crane.